IN THE HALL OF THE SAURIANS

PETER REDGROVE

Secker & Warburg
POETRY

First published in England 1987 by
Martin Secker & Warburg Limited
54 Poland Street, London WIV 3DF

Copyright © Peter Redgrove 1987

British Library Cataloguing in Publication Data
Redgrove, Peter
  In the hall of the Saurians.
  I. Title
  821'.914   PR6035.E267

ISBN 0-436-40997-6

Printed in Great Britain by
Biddles Ltd, Guildford and King's Lynn

CONTENTS

ACKNOWLEDGEMENTS

Acknowledgements are due to the following:

Ambit, *A Poet's 1982* (Poet & Printer), *London Review of Books*, *Manhattan Review*, *PN Review*, *Poetry* (Chicago), *Poetry Book Society New Year Supplement 1982*, *Poetry Book Society New Year Supplement 1983*, *Poetry Review*, *Prospice*, *Strawberry Fare*, *Temenos*, *Times Literary Supplement*, *2 plus 2*, *With a Poet's Eye* (Tate Gallery), *Words*

PNEUMONIA BLOUSES

The iron ships come in with hellish music
They are dedicated to golden oils and engines
And explosive riveting, their hulls heal
To tattoos of guns or iron drums, riveting.
And they worship the horse-mackerel and the sardine,
And why not, it is a living,
And a multitudinous beauty, that brings the souls in.
You see the machine-shop glitter in the tin,
They are water-moths flocking in their thousands;
The packers fit the silver engines in
Laid down in olive oil that is golden;
The key unwinds. Girls
In pneumonia blouses greet the fishermen
Whose balls are brimmed with nitroglycerine of souls,
In each lacy belly the embryo buoyant
As a nenuphar. In the sunlight
The old stone watches sweet and yellow as honeycomb.
Holding the milky child
Is like holding sleep in a bundle,
Which seeps everywhere. There is still frost
In the early morning shadows like spirit-photographs
And like the lace of girls in pneumonia blouses
Ruffled as are the wakes of working boats, fishermen's eyes
Open in all directions, but the shadows of night
Trawl them back again, the nets
Invisible in the black water.

HORSE LOOKING OVER
DRYSTONE WALL

---

for S.C.

A horse dips his nose into dry shadow
Gathered in the chinks like water.
He drinks the coastal dark
That dwells behind the wallstones
In the dry boulder caverns.

Light lies along his muzzle like a stone sheath.
From skull-darkness kin to the dry stone wall
The eyes watch like mirrors of stone;
This horse is half light, half dark,
Half flesh and half stone
Resting his silver muzzle on the shadowed wall
Like a horse made partly of the silver of clouds,

And partly it is a boulder with mane and nostrils
Watching over his wall the plentiful wild boulders
Maned with shaggy weed in galloping water which are kin,

Coralled boulders nostrilling under their manes and lathered
                                        with brine.

BELLS

Bells, the men are mending
The broken church-bells
In the silent church
Silent as a hollow cliff,
They clamber in linen-covered boots
Up and down the bells' mountains,
The chafing of their clambering boots
Produces from all the bells
A low sweet humming,
From the serious shape of bells
Their sound-look of sorrow
Like a tear swinging and crying
Crying and never falling;
The church with its note
That must be charged by bells,
Nave-tone that gathers
Gradually into audibility
Like a singing, and falls
Below the threshold of hearing

Unless it is rung and charged
By bells with true notes
And men with the changes right;
That prolongs the singing.
The men are repairing them.
Buds like birds sit perched
With tightly-folded wings,
The bush is like a silent church
Ready to sound.
In the cliff a great door of sunshine
Swings open and closes again
As the clouds scud: ice-grey chalk
Flooding with gold.

It is full of tuned chambers that are tiny shells
With ancient frosty tones, it is a milliard church,
And a flood-lit skull that goes dark;
A chalkface mirror
To sunshine, like a moon on earth; the child
Stands a moment in its light
And walks away inspired;
In the sun's heat
The crystals of chalk, the tiny fossils
In their billions
Have given off a tone
Like a bell mended by the sunlight.
The quarry nearby
Bears the open wound of the church
Ripped from its flank, in negative.

IN THE HALL OF
THE SAURIANS

In the Hall of Saurians, the light worked the bones,
The shadows stamped. I was haunted
With the heads colossal in death.
My father brought me here
In his bright shadowless car,
His jewel which he drives everywhere
As a coffin is lined in white satin
Brilliant in the darkness, like mother of pearl.

The wall of the Insect Gallery is splashed
In a butterfly shape with all the British Lepidoptera
And there are five times as many moths shown
For the Shadow in these times
Is correspondingly more significant than the Light.
What goes on in the darkness sees by perfume.
They say that to go out in the noon
Is to lose one's shadow,
To lose the moth of oneself.

My seed, my moth, was torn from me
Like gossamer in the wind
By the lady curator of all these bones,
Mistress of the Halls of Patterns of Death,
Keeper of the probable forms,
The underworld that is delivering constantly
The forms of life, at night like mud
That is a turreted museum, with endless galleries,
But at dawn, nevertheless,
The rainbow glides closer to us across the water
Until we stand within its coloured shells,
Its sequent halls. This is our form
Of transport, the ecstasy of these halls,

The forms displayed. My father in his jewel
Scurries away among the beetles.
The corpse of London transforms in his mouth,
His tales make of it a winged thing
Full of custom and surprise.
But these are winged buildings
As we make love after hours
In the Hall of the Saurians, and the flickering light
Works the bones and the shadows stomp
As up to a campfire smoky with jungle moths
To warm themselves or crush it out.

A FEW CARATS OF PAIN

The shadows were roaring
With pain on the other side of the mirror,
She pushed the glass up against the optic
But called the barman to draw my beer;
'You lose your grip,' she said,
'In rheumatoid arthritis, which is
Stone in the garden of the joints,'
She explained, and in the east wind
As if ice in the air were condensing on this stone,
Black ice; 'Verglas?' She agreed.

Welding in the glass,
Immovable joints under construction,
On the other side of the mirror
Shadows arced out on her face.
She served me chaser whisky anodyne
And the barman drew my beer in his firm grip.
'That's a handsome stone, my dear . . .'
'It's my life-savings, lover-boy,
Small as it is . . .' among the calcite flowers
Like an arc-tooth in the garden, refracting pain;
'You lose your grip at first
And no sign can be seen except the pain,
So I bought the diamond
To wear on my arthritic hand.' It was like
A folded window into the skin,
It was like a point of pain
Held on a gold band of concentration,
Its interior shadowless.

Her hand, she says, is a garden to this star
Which is a precipice when the east wind blows
And you lose your grip; you know your bones

In this disease, she says, outlined by pain,
'I've crowned this one like a King
With my life-savings . . .' she pushed
My glass up into the whisky-spring, and smiled;
Her perfume filled the bar, her story gripped us.

HER SHIRT OPEN

The great batholith under the soil.
The line of farms followed the springs
That leapt from the edge of this batholith.
They had built the town
On the remains of the plain
That was the ancient harbour silted up,
The plain of fine grey soil
That is a mixture of tiny shells
And granite dust. Behind the town
Were the great grey granite quays
From which the buildings had been quarried.

You could join the sea-people still, it was said,
By following the salty path.

I felt so active
With these changes in the living places,
With the rain springing up all around me.

She slipped with me into the alley
Which smelt of the good rain,
All the narrow streets of the town
Wound to that alley.
The rocking tides of perfume
That sprang from every slate and stone,
And the mass of static
The sun had piled up by beating
On that old stone, played everywhere
In its patterns like a sunshine from the earth,

Invisible sunshine and upward rain,
From the torrential earth
Its electrics leapt up the rain,
The pylon of rain.

She opens her shirt, which is wet
And heavy with its drink like a superb silk,
And an eerie feeling superimposes
From the stone electricity and that vertical smile,
Like another music, or echoes
Exploring buildings not yet visible,
The metallic echoes of the slate-lined alley
Erotic and holy, as when we watched
The slow-growing sea-drowned grass
And she turned to me again, her shirt open,
And the current changed around us, and in the canal
The underwater forests switched direction
Showing that sluices far away had opened up
New reaches of the waterway, with varying tides.

EDEN'S MEDICINE

for Alan and Su Bleakley

He had a taste in his mouth
Of early apple from Eden's medicine; wild-eyed
He regarded the thunder of heaven, its ominous
Independence; the deep sanity of the rock;
The happy madness of the marsh; the black roses
Of reference that root below the senses' reach;
The horse, the hooves ripping at the turf;
The flimsy and infinite child; the city
Curving round the train, inhaling train,
Exhaling train; a continued deep sound
Like a leather drum beaten softly, a wet
Bellows softly plied, the tide in the blowhole,
The sea breathing in the blowhole;
He saw like his own the eyes
Of fishes in the thunderstorm, the cold precision
Of ruched gold foil, pleated, unstormy, outlasting storms,
Open to all their troubles as the produce of the thundercloud
Smashes its mile-high windows all around
The fishmonger's glowing emporium:
For we call each other down
Into sleep by sharing images aloud,
As the bellies of the whales flood with fish,
Silver rivers of similitudes within;
The unweaned child smells of honeysuckle
In the nights, as you do. Catching thus
These images in the webs of our bodies,
Our embraces commingle, like magnetism
And we have put on just such an aerial tunic.
The centre does not stir, the pores open
Giving forth persuasion and affection, that began

In kisses woven together
Mingled in one robe like gossamer
From the Head even to the Feet; the two wheels
Of flashing silk enwrap each other,
Each drinks from the drinker at the root centre.

ABACUS

The oil from his shuffling fingers
Kept the abacus supple and in good condition,
The backbone of his business.

The lawn is listening
For the footsteps of its owner,
The vertebral footprints
Across the dew that shines
Like the cold moon spread thin.

Never draw on a sleeping person's face,
The bedewed spirit beaded like an arithmetician
Might not recognise herself when she returns;
It is wise, by the same token,
To repaint a departed person's room; and
People about to kill themselves start by redecorating, often.

We must minimise the ghostly portals and returns,
But what should we do with the abacus,
The supple abacus oiled
By a life-time's calculations? We ought
To incinerate the sweet-smelling juniper machine,
And send it after him through burning hinges,
To concrete the lawn and cobble it where he might print
Spiny footsteps on the necklace dew;
And do not face-paint, child, as you may doze:

(When we crayoned
Immense moustaches on sleeping Sari's face, she got up
And looked in the mirror and didn't know who it was,
And for days stayed dazed.)

AT THE COSH-SHOP

Hard rubber in its silk sheath like a nightie:
The assistant offered me a small equaliser,

A Soho Lawyer that could be holstered
In a specially-tailored back pocket,

And he would introduce me to his friend
The trouser-maker. I did not think this

Necessary, but I asked, Why the silk?
It seemed luxurious for such a hard argument.

Oh, Sir, so that it will draw no blood!
He seemed surprised I asked; I thought this not right;

I believe it was the blackness
The makers did not like to show,

Like an executioner it should draw on
Lily gloves, or like a catering waiter

For an instrument that performs a religious service,
Letting the ghost out temporarily with a shriek:

While all is peace within
They steal your worldly goods

Settling the argument by appeal
To deep non-consciousness

With a swift side-swipe, the Bejasus out of him –
Or an act of sexuality, equivalent?

Do the same people make the instrument
That will put the Bejasus back into a person?

The silk then would be the finest, for silk chafing
Hard rubber rouses electricity, it would be

Moulded to the individual sculpt of her lover,
Providing wisely for a longish trip, could seem

Dressed in his silk pyjamas, hard and tingling,
Or as the white silky cloud conceals the thunder

And the black current
That is going to shoot its white darts up and through.

CRAFT COUPLE
IN CORNWALL

A race run by the wind for a smock, all night. I see
You hanging out your dresses by the light of the moon.
Your husband has a beard like a bass brown humming
All over his cheeks. He crosses himself at a tiny piscina
With the figure of the Pieta in frosted glass, tit,
Brow, tit, left shoulder, right shoulder, left tit,
Brow, which is a star and not a cross, when he sees her
Hanging out her racing dresses in the breezes
Of moonlight. He makes a brooch: a vampire bat
Hugging a black obsidian to its pointed chest.

And this is the outcome of the struggle
Of the Church against the cult of water and the night sky:
Shaping a wet star in touch upon his torso. Stones
He knaps into their inner firmament, and plants
The flints round the garden in a star, where the dresses blow
And the flowers blow too, implicating all who come
In their perfume. I often see them
On his motorbike, iron maiden bellowing between his knees,
The roaring girl, his Black Goddess from Japan
Transporting her suppliants; on weekends in the town
They lose themselves in an arcade with 200 pinball
Machines. He often worships in the garden
At the piscina set into its flint wall,
These flints open too into their daylight blue,
Open like the flowers showing an inner sky
Which is perfumed, as her dresses are
From her inner sky, excited by their ride;
She pins them to the line without their aid.

She makes sinister pin-money as beautician
To the undertaker, and he remarks how shampoo
Never takes right on a corpse's hair
Unless her white hands zest the foam, and how
The dead draw down the flies, as if on strings,
Unless she washes them, and stars himself
At their privilege and funereal radiance.
Once they found an empty coffin beached
Like a rowboat on the mudbanks, and re-used it,
For love-letters and stock; it brims with brooches.
He hits on a new design, a Medusa-brooch,
With white hands on wriggling arms instead of snakes.

THUNDER-AND-LIGHTNING
POLKA

to J. H. Barclay

The fishmonger staring at the brass band
Offers us golden eyes from a cold slab
And silver instances of sea-flow. The birds

Which were dinosaurs once blanco the stone hats
Of pale admirals. The bandsmen puff their looping brass,
The music skating round and round its rinks

Of shiny tin, the hot trombones and the cool
And silvery horns, light
Sliding like the music along these pipes

And valves, curlicues and flaring tunnels,
Shells, instances of sonorous
Air-flow; we take a piece and present it

On the cold air to the staring ears
Of the sea fishmonger with his wet pets, our part
Of the hypersensitive cabaret. The river

Slides past all the feet; opal mud
Full of sunshine, some dead eye
Caresses the watery catacomb. A hot

Mailed fish has greased windows in the paper,
We eat to music. Above,
A cool high mountain of piled snow,

Its halls stuffed with thunderwork like wardrobes
Of black schoolmasters' gowns and lightning-canes,
White-painted; it turns to one immense

Black gown full of a booming voice from empty sleeves,
And shakes, and shakes its rain down,
And I kiss the thunder-water still booming in every drop

That strikes my face, I hear its flashing brass.
The bandsmen play on in their pavilion,
The instruments flash with lightning,

Their music is full of rain, and fate. I will not go indoors,
My sleeves are wet and heavy
Like velveteen; the trees are shaggy

With birds and lichen, singing in the leaves
In light tones and falling drops that break again
Like little thunder, and cold rain streams across

The wide golden eyes staring from the white slab.

WILD WALLS

(walls that swing aside on a film set)

The moon rises, hanging granite mirror.
The puff ball, of its own shape,
Smokes with love in the wind.

Out of its rent, its tear,
Its split side, its bloodless wound,
All of it
Is turning to seed, spending itself
Along the wind, lodging itself
Everywhere like the gossamer
Of October ploughed fields
That make steely pathways
To the moon, being flossed
With gossamer that shines;
Thoroughly flossed, layer upon layer.

Where have the spiders gone in their seeding tribes?
Into the wild walls of the browning woods
Like puffball smoke,
The trees thin in their yellow-reds
Like huge bonfires blowing on either side.
The wave of autumn pours in
Roaring and trailing its pomps,
The moon rises, reflecting whole yellows, reds,
In its granite mirror that hangs high, and higher.

INTO THE ROTHKO
INSTALLATION

(Tate Gallery, London)

Dipping into the Tate
As with the bucket of oneself into a well
Of colour and odour, to smell the pictures
And the people steaming in front of the pictures,
To sniff up the odours of the colours, which are
The fragrances of people excited by the pictures;
As the pair walk down the gallery
On each side of them the Turners glow
As though they both were carrying radiance
In a lantern whose rays filled the hall like wings
That brushed the images, which glowed;

Into the Installation, which smells
Of lacquered canvas soaking up all fragrance,
Of cold stone, and her scent falters
Like cloth torn in front of the Rothkos
Which are the after-images of a door slammed
So blinding-white the artist must shut his eyes
And paint the colours floating in his darkness.

He chose the darkest of the images for that white,
That green; red on red beating to the point
Where the eye gasps, and gives up its perfume
Like a night-flowering plant; and with many
Thin washes he achieves the effect
Of a hidden light source which smells
Like water far off in the night, the eye
So parched; paintings you almost can't see;

21

As if in painting
The Israelites crossing the Red Sea
He painted the whole wall red, and,
Black on black therein,
God somewhat like a lintel. We brought
The lanterns of ourselves in here
And your imagination blotted our light up, Rothko;
The black reached out, quenching our perfume
As in a dark chapel, dark with torn pall,
And our eyes were lead, sinking
Into that darkness all humans have for company;

Standing there, eyes wide, her lids faltered
And closed, and 'I see it, now' she said
And in her breath a wonderful blaze
Of colour of her self-smell
Where she saw that spirit-brightness
Of a door slammed open, and a certain green insertion
Shifting as her gaze searched
What seemed like a meadow through the white door
Made of lightning, cloud or flowers, like Venusberg
Opening white portals in the green mountain
Stuffed with light, he having used
The darkest of all that spectrum almost to blindness

And in his studio in the thin chalk of dawn
Having passed inwardly through that blackness,
Slitting his wrists, by process of red on red
He entered the chapel under the haunted mound
Where the white lightning of another world
Flashed, and built pillars. We left
The gallery of pictures rocked
By the perfume of a slammed eye, its corridors
Were wreathed with the detonation of all its pictures
In the quick of the eye, delighting into
Perfumes like fresh halls of crowded festival.

PLAYING DEAD

His dead-white face,
The eyelids of chalk
With the bold black cross marked

Cancelling the eyes, declaring
Hollow-socketed death, and the
Marble-white countenance

Declaring death
And the red nose to admit
He had died drinking

And the vertical eyelid-stripe
Telling us not only can he open
His eyes up and down but also

From side to side in the stare
Of a real ghost
Who does as he likes

Because Death breaks all the rules, and is
At very best an outrageous joke, and almost
Whatever Death does is quite soon forgotten;

So the Clown pratfalls on the skeleton
Of a banana, and two well-dressed Clowns
Accelerate with custard pies their mutual putrefaction,

As if it were funny to worry overmuch
About these bodies we wear like increasingly
Baggy pants with enormous knucklebuttons, especially
If like that sepulchral makeup they wipe off
In cold cream to white sheer speechless laughter.

A LOVER

to M.

Heavy magic sobs. They take omens
From the children's shouts playing near the Church.
The funeral is a way of preventing the formation

Of a lingering ghost. Stars
Linking down into the water
Among the lights of boats. Lift the Hare

And its fur is full of colour, it scurries
Through heath fires to confuse the scent.
She dazzled him with her blouse, dandled

Him in the bosom of it, the swooping front.
He thought he heard
Heavy magic sobs inside, from the heavy breasts

That swung as she walked, like two animals
Impassioned, trying to escape; her sweet smile
Above. She offered him

The whisky bottle, the shadowed bottle
Of dark glass. He felt the wells
Of friendship rising towards her, and they drank

Their dark spirit among the shadowed nettles,
Their waxes and poisonous greases. The children's shouts
Came floating over the common grass, which looked

Dusty and stale, as if it had not slept.
This is what it was like at Lodestone, with my grannie
Who was my parents, the stars linking down

Into the water, the hilly meadows
Where the hares box, where they
Dazzle us with everything created, outside

My grannie's dark kitchen, the houses
Standing open to the world, the hares boxing
On a thousand hills. She had a voice

Like a house, capacious, and with many
Cupboards, under the five-fingered stars,
And a blouse in which the breasts dazzled and boxed.

THE BIBLE BEHIND
THE SCENE

The dog trotting criss-cross
Nipping at the cows
To keep them on their road, heavy mothers,
And the slow pendulum of their milk
Would tip them into the ditch without the dog,
Without the thin boy with the peeled wand
Directing with light taps, and the old cowman
Trudging with his face of tanned cowhide.
The leather bible, the bible behind the scene,
The bible behind everything,
To open a book that leads away from happiness,

That opens on blackness and massacres and black endpapers,
On blackness like an airlock; breath rushes out.

The great house, built with the bible. We visit in
The season of the massacre of the rooks, that witch-hunt.
They are too black and gregarious to find safe hiding.
The smell of rain drifts into the drawing-room,
The tubby polite man with the family face
Expounds the family portraits, swings open
The family bible, whose rook-tree
Of ancestors gone to fill the pictures
Smells of mildew and sawdust, tranquillity. We gaze
At the fields of wild mustard that gaze back
Full of honeybees like a purring cat's stare.
The thin boy sticks his withy
Back into a hedge, it is almost the hour
When Pan sleeps, the cowman cracking poppy-seeds
Like a house of sleepy heads between his teeth.

A DEWY GARMENT

The shower witheld matures to thunder,
Such activity, then such rest;
I walk out in my worm-coloured shoes
Through the puddles where the worms luxuriate,
The bone-coloured worms
In the fallen skies of the puddles;
My love of thundershowers was given to me
By Odeon University:
Such downpours in the tropical forests,
The great leaves catching the rain by its lips
Hanging poised in banquets,
And the repose was as wide as the blank screen
Still crossed by the images.
And there was never a storm without a wet girl
Shiny in drenched tropicals
Flickering to those lightnings, submitting to Tarzan,
And the film a black-and-white thunderstorm
Flashing eighteen times a second,
Which welded its lights to a seamless narrative,
For the demonic or the divine is the sudden,
And the cinema soothes the sudden.
Katharos, the putting on of a fresh garment
Even of jungle-grass
After soil and toil, the repose
In a fresh garment clean as an imagery screen,
This skin across which the thunder has played,
This skin
Of discharged rain and stretches of water;
A dewy garment covers me,
Restless manhood is gone.

CONCERNING DREAMS

He dreamed of getting into a large white car
Of a sporty kind.
That is getting into the lunar mode, he cried,
The mode of the passion-flower, the perfumed mode.

Indeed, he said, when he opened the door,
The interior is full of a marvellous
Scent of fresh flowers;

Concerning dreams,
He tries to remember what the old folk said
And this stills his thought for a while, with
Some piece of this or the other knowledge;
'But still the earth on which we drive is not finished,'
He protests, 'Do you not feel how it bumps and shakes?'

THE GIRL READING
MY POETRY

This is an impossible event!
This melody is my extensive lechery –
The girl reading my poetry
Launders it;
An impossible accomplishment!
Cleansed white, in London –
The beauty distilled of this dreck
Washed in a maidenly mouth . . .

And moreover the audience
From the facing 200 gilt chairs
Witnessing the ablution
Stay entirely quiet,

And as they warm to the mouth of this new muse
Give off first a perfume in the breath,
Then from their entire tapestry of skin
So that
I cannot believe this blossoming,
Like a baby fresh from its bath,
Like flowers nodding
In the quickened breath
Along the polite rows –

And then they spatter it by applause,
The fast detonations of applause,
The rattle of musketry in a flowering garden!
They charge it with kinesis
And propel it like bullets
With bravo and encomium –

And she stands there spattered with it
And glowing with the fine smell,
And takes her smiling breath
Of the cloud of quelques fleurs and cordite
And drinks up these chemicals and the electricity
Generated by applause inside the invisible
Air-hued cloud of alchemy
And imagery poetry-gas.

Overwhelmed and saturated by this opera
I glance at my printed words,
They are a taciturn libretto,
Yet I must have said something right,
My own smell small like a damp railway station,
The iron-flavoured air of it waiting for the local train:

While she, and they,
Were like the express roaring into Truro,
The doors shooting open, the holiday plumage alighting,
Boarding, the terrace of doors slamming,
And the whole symphony rowing up the line out of my ken,
Articulating with its rolling stock and its headlights blazing.

A MAZE LIKE US

The lightning zig-zags through its maze.
The thunderbird takes feathers of blue flame,
Flaps immense shadows in his mountain aviary
Of clouds, immense lightnings
Among the heaped water, the heavenly
Cisterns with their gunpowder disposition
That are in this moment sapphire,

This moment, ebony scented with electricity.
There is a darkness that reveals other lights
Present in this thunderstorm, present in the mother
Of clouds. I switch on the electric fan
In the sultry heat and the air is
Folded, escaping billows of ether.

In the bushes the great ethers
Of a hare's body rotting as though
That body of death were exploding
In rainbows and the thunderstorm
Is putrefaction's fast mode. The thundershower

Is suddenly solid in the window behind you
And your face changes, your speech falters,
The room's mode shifts, the sub-light switches
On and off in the hiss and the aah; on that curtain
Of water there is a rainbow shone
By the house-lights, within its purple, a wash
Of rainbow. The blue-eyed thunder
With the drenched hair, and the secret place
In the bend of the cloud where
The serpent-lightning sneaks, the fire-snake,

The twist in the maze
And the blindend where something waits
In the void behind the cloud,
Where she conceals herself, zig-zagger.

THE MOONS OF SCILLY

For S.C.

Grounded moons, a scrapheap
Of discarded moons, every one a beauty.
Sealed stone boilers of seaweed machines,
The stones that power the boiling spume-engines,
They are pulled by their great fellow-stone

In the sky that swoops low
And clocks them together,
That pulls the waves up against the cliffs
In great momentary ferns
And sends the shocks deep into their hearts

Where pictures form that glow for ages.

The cliffs are full of such pictures
Packed like recordings of these shaped shocks,
Millennial libraries of stone audios.

But you'd not know it from this stillness
In a palm-of-the-hand stone-meadow beach.
The sky is made of stone also.
There are many cracks in this palm from hard labour,
Turning the sea over and over;

The cracks in the stones are so deep
They look like iron straps. The shadows from the sky
Lie on the land so hard they deepen into cracks,
A palm seamed by slow action.

Some thunder-lizards retiring from time
Have become their eggs again.
They have rolled themselves up into their crocodilian
                                                    beginnings.

This shore is the skin of an egg too big to see.

The sands of all the deserts have formed into one single
                                                    fractured grain.

There are many broken stone torsos.
There is a great sphinx of rucked stone and closed eyes.

Lichens open like little scrolls all over its stone lids,
Lichen-books, library of sea-shocks, cloud-bursts.

And a wrecked boat on a stone foreshore becoming stone;
It has been there so long it has caught stone,
Infectious whiteness, deeply gorgonised,
The ground of pebbles its unyielding ocean.

LUNAR MANE

As a mane of hair to a comb
Or a cat to thunder, so the loose
Chafing clothes charge the lady up
And her fragrances pile at collar, cuffs and
Hem of the skirt, like that low smell
That comes off a lawn just before the rain falls;
Low thunder and flashes of lightning
Emitted by her in lunar cycle; the rich clouds
Pass over the full moon; like an electrical engine
That is made of flesh and blood,
From the men a brooding tension that cannot earth
Without her. She watches the retort of the bird's beak
Dropping shining seeds, fruit-wet. The seeds
Polish their husks in the bird-guts, the clouds
Hang unsatisfactorily, like crooked pictures, the plants,
Striving for adjustment, turn about their centres;
She now in riding-gear, animated with the sweat of horses,
Seeds of power glistening in the wet mane,
Tossing out rainbows. The big wheels of the shelving wind
As she leaps over the hedge of flowers that are opening,
The crooked thundercloud as low as it dares . . .
(A fly on my wrist reading my notes, like horse
And rider in one, stout with eggs in its panniers
And dabbing its tongue where my pulse beats.)

FAR STAR

It is like living in a transistor with all this radio
Which is the inner weather of the house
Presided over by housegoddesses who turn
Everything that happens into perfume and electricity;
Oh! she cries, what a blessing – and I smell the blessing
Like a candle lighted, a scented flame that spreads
Through closed doors, opening them;
And when she curses, sulphur blackens all the knives.
We have tuned our circuits by living together so long
And the child, never having known another house, deepest
                                                         tuned:
She was broadcast into this world via the lady transmitter
And mostly plays musical comedy, though now is of an age
For an occasional tragic aria about the sister she has not got,
Who will not now be broadcast from that far star;

And I wish heartily we had more loos – our tuning is such
On the same channel that we all three must shit
                                                simultaneously.

LOCAL CELEBRATION

I

The sun's lightning caught in the sea's powerhouse,
The great wheel turning and turning slowly,
The great wheel cogged with its foaming coasts.
The blowhole:
The white shadow hanging over the black cliff
Like a ghost hovering over a spiritualist,
The ghost of a white horse;
The moist nostril of the sea smoking and snorting.
On the little wavelets the masts of the yachts
Flicker like galvanometer needles,
Clanking their cleats. On the rocks
There is a gingham party,
The table-cloth spread, gingham, and the fruits.
One of the girls in Sunday mood remarks
That Jesus transfigured the womb. Her friend's rejoinder:
That a woman's virginity is only truly taken
By her own labour.

II

There is one dog, shared by all the girls,
And he is father of the castle pups. He is
Venerable, a pattern and a meditator:
No gingham, no boots or books,
A simple basket, diffusing cordial hormones
From his warm back, like a sage
Wrapped in an animal skin; a sage who yet
For toilet paper employs his supple tongue.

III

On the old oak table in the castle wardroom shines
A marvel: an anchor from a ship lost
In the December storms, but scoured papery-thin
And worried silver-bright by the black gravel bottom.
The hour is signalled from the parapets
By the evening cannon firing, like
A small charge of powder detonated to greet a great god.

IV

There are caverns and tunnels in the castle hill.
At sunset, while the loaves and fruit
Are being packed away, from these caves
And re-entrants come flapping sounds and cawing
As though under the hill lived enormous birds: it is the tide
Turning at the month's end, the day when there is
Only the one tide.

V

As the moon rises, the girls
Pack away their gingham dresses
Into the hampers, with the food,
To be naked as their shadows;
Supping the leggy night-melons,
Burying their faces in the between-leg dark,
Nuzzling the lunar slice; the deep sea
Building, in its dark, towering linings
Of chalk, the black dog of tides
This way, that, pawing stertorous shingle.

A SCARECROW

A scarecrow in the field,
Dressed like a King
In streamers of tinfoil
Which flash in the sun
And glitter;

And in the deep night
As the moon rises
That glittering again
Appears in the field
As if a fountain
Were standing guard
Over the furrows;

A tattering robe
Of strips of tinfoil
Ragged and gorgeous because
Of its liquid facility with the light,
And so multiplex

That it is a squadron riding
With swords out saluting the light.

The birds rejoice with their song
At this wonder of the sun
Willowing on its cross-pole,
And in this presence of the moon
Raggedy in the fertile field,
And nip therefore their share only
Of seeds sown out of the loam,
And do not multiply their kind
Desperately being content seemingly
That an alchemical balance has been achieved:

The tinfoil rebus in the open field.
Even the vicar, passing the scarecrow field
Is reminded of life
That is not only dust to dust
But light to light and air to air,
Shooting his cuffs,
Flashing his watch.

WET PINUP

Great feathers of tide spreading to the horizons
At the Saltings; noisy discos
On stout pillars of water-light stand blaring;
Voyagers with the vehemence of their lovemaking
In the harbour rock their tethered boats' reflections;
Water-butchers ply trim craft, on land
They are fishmongers in white
With gilt-lettered shops & Son and marble slabs,
At sea they are dressed in nothing but fish-blood;
A sea-conch like an unbroken note; for we are all
Brothers and sisters of the sea; throw the pebble
Back into the tide and let it resume its work
Of self-making in the common womb. The waterman

Opens feathers in the deep, his speedboat chalks
Swift white water-marks across the whole visible ocean
In great scorings like skaters and like the marks
Of airliners over the glassy sky, feather-voyagings.
And she wears such a wake, to be so wet
Is to be part of the sea, an intensification of it,
An unbroken note, her smile and her skirts
Conching about her shelly hips, her tits
Gazing wide-eyed through the tendril-clinging blouse
Like a sea-soaked bough of blossom, for her perfumes

Hunt close to her like beasts crouched so low
As to be incredible in the water between us; I believe
If you could see these fit animals they would resemble
Electric eels so charged they're feathered; and tits
Like spiralling grain bud-knotted.

DRY PARROT

The Parrot of Warlock's Wood,
Of Peter's Wood,
It leaves wide twiggy footprints,
It walks in its cinder wings
Like a tight-buttoned fellow
In oyster-grey tailcoat;

A Parrot has no blood
Only calcium filings,
It dries a room;
Peter keeps the Parrot
To dry the house out;
It was a clinker egg
Before it was a thirsty Parrot.

Now it taps on the clear dry mirror
And with its beak begins
To loosen the mummy plumage
And shake the egg-sand out
And utters an Egyptian cry and flies
Taking to the air up the chimney
Like a roaring hearth-fire
In its anhydrous glory.

WINE

It is a loving thing

It exhales its sweet breath
As I uncork the bottle
The room is filling with its spirit-breath

One flesh with my own,
The little row of fountains
Uncorks in my mouth.

I drink
And become an ordinary maniac

Wine is a loving thing

It coils an invisible vine
Which wreathes about us,
Leopards approach, white leopards
(The smell of this wine, the hiss
Of the tree in the Garden of Eden,
The half-moon bouquet of the bitten fruit.)

A BOYISH MOULD

A water-spaniel named 'Dream'.
The wet-footed snail with its sun-dry stone on its shoulders,
Pebble house, gravestone pack, pebble knapsack,
Hollow rock, livingstone. A boy's feast:
Sausages and tinned pineapple; and after,
Racing the Snails: the milestones glide.

The clunchbuilt church with a Doom Window
Of the sorting of souls, and the reputed tree
On which they hanged men, for it left
Something sad in the soil, something sour
So no grass would grow.

Only certain mushrooms
Eaten under the hangman's tree for a special dare,
And the hanged men came conjured
To the boys' feast
Like uncles, like magic uncles.

And one boy who had cut his leg
Was made for life,
For a bony uncle handed him
Mould from a bark to press on his wound,

And called it by a magic name
In the mouldy lingo of the mossy jaws,
Sounding of pocketmoney, the precise sum
Of a penny and a shilling,
And this name became
The boy's blazon. This is the story
As I prefer it of the great discovery:

For as long as I take pocketmoney,
He told his father,
I will take no more than this,
I will take a shilling and a penny,
A Penny-shilling. The scar was silver-clean
Like living stone.

A pallid straw-field of stubble,
A bleached field,
A raven stalking through
Like a robed schoolmaster
Planting his feet squarely
On stones of law,
Invisible stones,
Through an uneventful field.
The raven in its frock coat
Plants its step
Like a small lamp
That dirties what it shines upon
Pecking at the light
With a quickpitch shadow,
Like our earth
Tending at anchor,
Moored to the bright sun,
Sending out into infinite space
On its night-side a pecking shadow.
The raven paces out
Under the great
Radio ears like umbrella bones

Tilted over the bleached fields.
What colour is radio, what
Do they message, can they see
A raven marching among the husks,
What food do they find for it
In the glare of their night?

It is said
A raven is born
Every time it thunders
Over the wheat-fields
Golden as kippers;
That thundercloud pecking with radio
In the sunset which tinctures
With light that we can see,
Light like gold-leaf on an elephant:
A black alchemist
In his golden robes;
I wish Telstar would read the thunder.

Radio pours into the atmosphere
And the raven visits, it should not surprise
If the radio transformations turn his progeny
Inside out
So they have golden feathers then
And eyes like thunder, their father.

SUNLIGHT, MOONLIGHT, STONELIGHT

(Scillies)

A heath of turf that bows to the sea at night,
A webwork of sunshine in which the islands are caught;
A black cliff still as a sleeping medium throws out its white
                                                    cloud-ghost
Miles into the air. The sea contains more lights
Than the sky does, by millions, in fractured waves.

Smaller ghosts are raised on the low rocks
By the continual deaths of the waves
On a beach of stone tied deeply with streams of erosion,
With iron clamps of shadow. Doorways
Open a crack in the stone. There is light within,
But not the kind of light we can see with.
Limpets crawl to bask in it there, the mussels jostle
The barnacles. The sea breaks casks
Of white light that searches and mingles
Into the blacklight cracks of the stone. The light of the sea
Chalked on stone coasts by a stone moon,
By the waves of a stone moon,
The rolling casks full of white spume

Is a reasoning, active light; the light of the stone

Ponders only one image, that of stone,
Which is presence more than image,
A back-shock and a spindrift cuff, or high and dry
In its massif, voiding a sky-clambering ghost,
Or pelvis of itself, throne of its own foetus,
Squeezed by the tide weeping an electrical note.

The water becomes black and will not send back any images.

A star touches the water, the whole sea
Becomes a cog of tines, a clock of dancing cogs, then the
                                                    faint-gold
Touch of the star goes and the sea
Is a restless liquid full of self-lighted stones.

BEES AT CHALICEWELL

(Glastonbury)

The many bees drink from this garden well,
Alight on leaf-rafts, and kneel, drinking,

They hover in the brick shaft
And the echoes buzz in its round tower

Above its darkened amber-black surface
Richly-nubbed with thirsty bee that drinks also

From the rain-soaked yew, the great water-head,
The stemmed well of water spitted by needles,

Tree of stabbed drops; the bees kneel
To the great yew, and push their heads

Into the drops, and drink,
And from the wet skins

Of the big round clean stones
Drink, and from the driblets

Of the religious chalybeate stream
That speeds through the private gardens,

The well-chalice gardens
Where contemporary pilgrims linger

And stare into the pool too long
Changing the water's taste,

Who leave their faces in the water
Their tongues licking the parched

Lips of the images, round and round.

WAITING FOR FLOOD-TIME

The birds turning invisible pages over and over.
The rooks caw, building up arches of sound,
Arches where they live together,

Flowing arches of stone, and branch,
And their shadows, and their echoes,
Stone homes and echo-houses.

On a still, curled leaf
A brownbottle of autumn sipping,
A winged brown bottle of autumn juice

Hatched in the momentary beam of heat
Shot off the mirror-cold sea
As the sun lies down in that mercurial chill

And quenches itself to a pale yellow air.
Winter is made of sheet-metal shadows,
Where there is shade there is ice.

The flood Sundays will come,
'Parson riding stirrup-deep over the flooded bridge';
Mild Lazarus greets him, his bony arms full of flowers.

THE BIG SLEEP

Sea, great sleepy
Syrup easing round the point, toiling
In two dials, like cogs

Of an immense sea-clock,
One roping in, the other out.
Salt honey, restless in its comb,

Ever-living, moving, salt sleep,
Sandy like the grains at eyes' corners
Of waking, or sleepiness, or ever-sleeping;

And when the sun shines, visited as by bees
Of the sun that glitter, and hum in every wave,
As though the honey collected the bees;

The honey that was before all flowers, sleepiness,
Deep gulfs of it, more of it than anything,
Except sleepy warm rock in the earth centre

Turning over slowly, creating magnetism,
Which is a kind of sleepiness, drowsy glue
Binding the fingers, weakly waking fingers,

Or fingers twitching lightly with the tides;
And the giant clock glides like portals, tics
Like eyelids of giants sleeping, and we lie

In Falmouth like many in a bed,
And when the big one turns
We all turn; some of us

Fall out of bed into the deep soil,
Our bones twitch to the tides,
Laid in their magnetic pattern, our waters

Rise like white spirits distilled by the moon,
Can get no further, and turn over
Heavy as honey into the sea

To sleep and dream, and when the big one dreams
We all dream. And when she storms
We all weep and ache, and some fall

Into her gulfs as she tosses, and we weep
For the lifeboats toiling on the nightmares . . .
But in those beds waters touch each other

Coiling, in a certain way, and where they touch,
At the very point, a mineral spark,
A bone begins to grow, someone is

Putting bones together in the gulf,
In her accustomed patterns – and in their season
The women walk about the town, a big drop

Of the Dreamer in their bellies, and in the drop
A smaller dreamer, image of themselves,
Who are the image dreamed by the ocean's drop,

By the two clocks, one roping in, one out.